Published by Stratford Living Publishing.

ISBN Print: 978-1-990332-58-6

Dedicated to Cheryl

The other night at dinner...

Mom served
something new.

It tasted like roast beef...

But it really made me chew!

My tummy felt funny...

So I went to lie down in my room...

My older brother followed me...

He asked, "What's all the gloom?"

I said my tummy felt funny...

I rubbed it as you do.

My brother laughed and pointed at my head...

He said, "You've got a HARE IN YOUR HAIR!"

I hopped out of bed!

Hitting my head harder than I expected to...

Yelling at the top of my lungs I had to...

JUMP, JUMP, JUMP AND SAY THERE'S A HARE IN MY HAIR!

"Get it out! Get it out!" I shouted.

My brother told me the hare was there because I ate its cousin!

I'm not a baby, but I began to cry.

I was frightened and shook like a leaf.

"Try to sleep,"
my brother said with a
grin.

It was so quiet you could hear the drop of a pin.

The hare ran around my scalp so I had to...

JUMP JUMP JUMP AND SAY THERE'S A HARE IN MY HAIR!

"I was only kidding," my brother teased.

But I still believed it to be true.

"It's all in your imagination," he said but still I had to...

JUMP JUMP JUMP AND SAY THERE'S A HARE IN MY HAIR!

Mommy and Daddy came into my room...

Dad asked, "What's all the fuss?"

Mommy patted me on the head...

She said, "Darling, your hair is all mussed!"

The hare hopped around and around

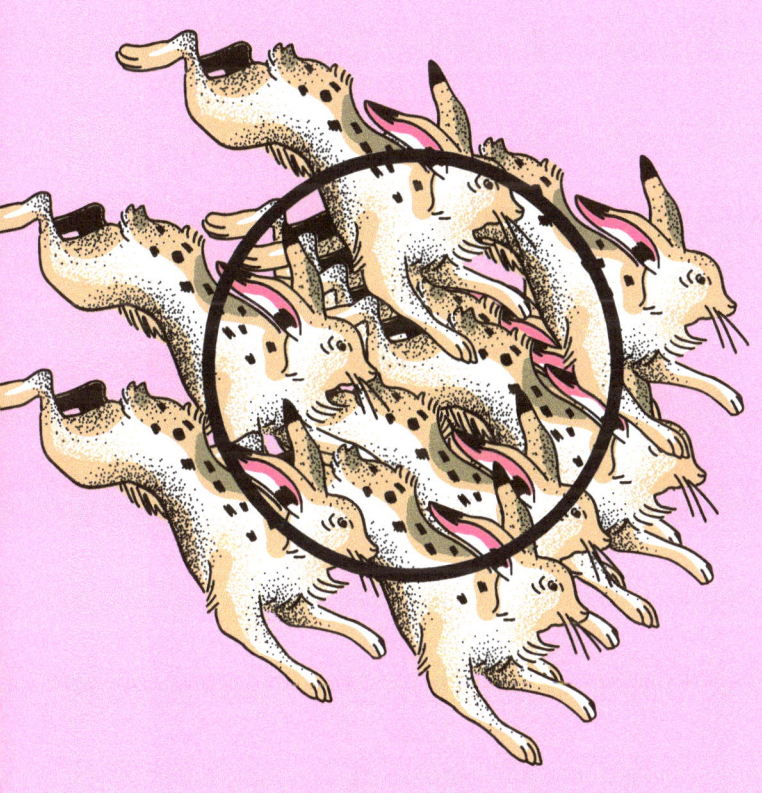

Like he was lost and trying to be found.

Mommy said,
"Darling, stop your hair from moving around."

"I can't,"
I said with a frown.

"Of course you can," Daddy coaxed.

But Mommy knew
my brother
loved his own jokes.

"What did you do?" she asked as I began to...

JUMP, JUMP JUMP AND SAY THERE'S A HARE IN MY HAIR!

My brother laughed and lurked...

Daddy said,
"As lies go, son,
this is your worst!"

Finally my brother apologized for telling me lies.

Ashamed, he even covered his eyes.

But I could still feel that crazy hare...

Even though he said
there was
no hare there!

Mommy tried to calm me down by combing my hair

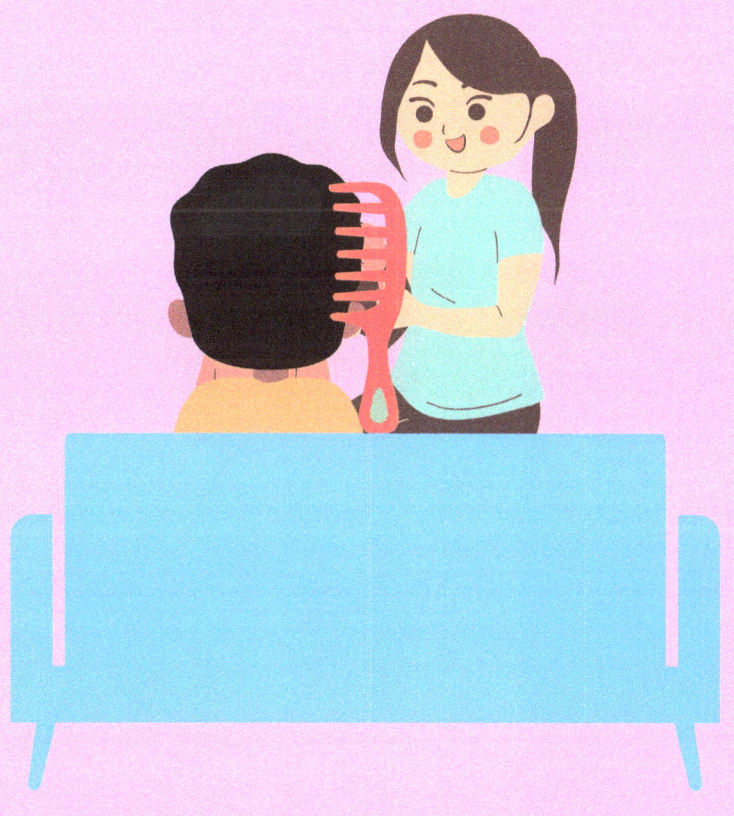

While my brother hid quietly inside his hood...

Then we understood..,

We laughed and stared when my brother began to...

JUMP JUMP JUMP BECAUSE THERE WERE HARES IN HIS HAIR!

We don't

HARE
IN OUR
HAIR!

Other books in the
Jump Series:
Jump Like a Caribou!
Jump Like a Kangaroo!
Jump at the Zoo!
Jump and Say P.U.!
Jump and Say Boo!
Jump and Say Valentine's Day Is
For Kids Too!
Jump and Look For a Clue
Jump and Say Happy Birthday to
You!
Jump For Everything Blue!
Jump and Say Cock-A-Doodle-Do!

Jump and Squawk Like a Cockatoo!
Jump and Ask Is It Ewe?
Jump and Say There's an Ewww in My Stew!
Jump and Cheer Happy New Year!
Jump, Hop and Say Happy Easter To You!
Jump and Say There's A Moo-Moo In My Tutu!

The Three Boulders
Billy Shakespeare
Billie Shakespeare

NON-FICTION
103 Fundraising Ideas For Parent Volunteers With Schools and Teams